Bloom

Anesha Pandor

authorHOUSE®

AuthorHouse™ UK
1663 Liberty Drive
Bloomington, IN 47403 USA
www.authorhouse.co.uk
Phone: 0800.197.4150

Published by AuthorHouse 11/24/2017

ISBN: 978-1-5462-8227-3 (sc)
ISBN: 978-1-5462-8226-6 (e)

In the name of Allah, the Most Gracious, The Most Merciful.

Introduction

This book is filled with short but deep spiritual insights and personal reflections. These insights came to me whilst on my own personal spiritual journey.

I now hope to share these insights and reflections to help heal, awaken and inspire others.

These daily insights and reflections fall under the months of the seasonal year.

This is because in order for a flower to bloom, one must plant the seeds first, then water it, and then nurture it with the right conditions.

'Blooming' is a gradual process and nature is always the best teacher. As the philosopher Lao Tzu once said, 'Nature does not rush, yet everything is accomplished'.

You will also notice that these insights and reflections are not in any thematic order.

They fall under various categories, such as love, hope, faith, wisdom and more.

This is to keep it free flowing and natural, as the way they were inspired.

At various points, I use the word 'God' and in some instances I use the word 'Allah' when mentioning a 'higher power'.

Please feel free to use a word that comes naturally to you in the moment.

Wishing all my readers lots of love, light and peace, and may you find the beauty and confidence within you to bloom into your best self.

Love,

Anesha x

When you need reminding of your beauty,
go stare at the flower—
For in its reflection will be your true essence
reflected back to you.

January

January 1

Let go of your need for life to go according to your plan, and let it go according to God's plan.

January 2

The first step to getting the things you want
in life is this: decide what you want.

January 3

The answers are not elsewhere; they are within.

January 4

Write.

Write as if no one is reading. Lay your soul bare.

January 5

We are all born special. Some just don't know it yet.

January 6

Let the prisoner in your heart go free.

January 7

When you think you are worth nothing, remember
that the God who created the stars, the sun,
and the moon is the same God who created
you. You are worth more than you think.

January 8

Fall in love with your flaws, and
call them quirks instead.

January 9

Your destiny is greater than what you see.

January 10

Maybe peace is found within the struggle
and not outside it. Maybe healing is found
in the pain and not the cure outside it.

January 11

If you go in search of the truth, it
will be made clear to you.

January 12

Let go of goals, and strive for a purpose.

January 13

Find God through your heart and not just
through your head. You can find God through
logic, but you feel Him within your heart.

January 14

Grow from a place of fullness.

January 15

You forget your purpose when you forget your origin.

January 16

When a moment of happiness comes to you,
feel it. Be present in it. Give gratitude for it;
appreciate it. But don't get attached to it.

January 17

The wounds that are never healed will always come
to the surface. Spend the time to heal them.

January 18

You ruin the present by worrying about the future.

January 19

The best thing to become is yourself.

January 20

I am beautiful, the world is beautiful, and people
are beautiful. Beauty is everywhere. Repeat
until you feel the radiant energy within.

January 21

The deeper the roots, the sturdier the tree.

January 22

When you change yourself, you change the world.

January 23

Cherish the journey; that's where the miracles happen. The destination is simply the prize.

January 24

Be the light that lights the way for others.

January 25

Your purpose is to become who you really are.

January 26

The less you carry on your shoulders, the higher you fly.

January 27

Don't be so focused on working for the future that you forget to live and enjoy the present.

January 28

Focus on your intentions, and the
outcome will take care of itself.

January 29

Why wait until tomorrow when
tomorrow is not guaranteed?

January 30

Trust God. Trust your future.

January 31

The greatest gift you can give your soul is
to know and connect to its Creator.

February

February 1

Shine so brightly that the stars get jealous.

February 2

True love appears in your darkest
moments and shows you the light.

February 3

Be your own best friend.

February 4

Even if you have only a little love to give,
give it all. Love never depletes. The more you
give of your heart, the more it grows.

February 5

Believe that God is going to give you something
beyond your expectations. Be hopeful.

February 6

If you are pleasing God, you will find peace.

February 7

Do not settle for anyone who does not
accept you for all that you are.

February 8

True love happens when you are not just ready to give love but when you are ready to receive it.

February 9

Some people can only reach the stars by falling. It's only by falling that you can find the strength to rise higher than before.

February 10

Your year will come – a time when you
will find your wings and fly.

February 11

You can survive on your own, but you weren't created to survive alone. God created a partner for you so that together you can survive the storm.

February 12

'I was tired of being the thorn, so I decided to become the rose.'

February 13

If love is inside you, it will find you.

February 14

The best type of love is the love that starts
slowly but touches deeply. A love that
starts fast usually ends just as fast.

February 15

Your purpose is to be here in this moment, fully present.

Burn the pieces of yourself that are not you, so you can give birth to the pieces that are you.

February 17

It's not about how fast you go, but where you finish.

February 18

Maybe life's not about having all the answers.
It's about putting your trust in God and
going with the flow of your heartbeat.

By giving love you are teaching love.

February 20

The little things you do for people – they matter.

February 21

Sometimes it's more painful not to light
the candle than it is to let it burn.

February 22

Trust that your heart's longing will be fulfilled.

February 23

You are a creation of God, so treat yourself
with kindness, compassion, and respect.

February 24

The best way to find yourself is to
get lost in a higher purpose.

February 25

'I will find myself, I will find my way.'

February 26

Love every part of yourself, so you
can love every part of another.

February 27

You can't choose love and fear at the same time. Choose the one you want.

February 28

You can't accept the gifts of your future if you
are holding on to the pain of the past.

February 29

Bloom – where you are, just as you are.

March

March 1

If there was no such as a right or wrong
decision, what would you choose?

March 2

With every step I take, I am getting
closer to my path and purpose.

March 3

All art is an expression of love.

March 4

Strive for growth, not for success.

March 5

Maybe it's not always about searching and finding. Maybe it's about accepting.

March 6

Every morning ask yourself, 'What do I want to do?" – not what you should do. And then go do it.

March 7

All the love you seek is within you.

March 8

Nothing happens by accident.
Everything serves a purpose.

March 9

There is goodness in every situation you
are in because God chose it for you.

March 10

The present moment is perfect.

March 11

When you start sharing the greatness and beauty within you, others will follow you.

March 12

Your opinion of yourself matters the most.

March 13

Instead of searching for true love, let
true love reveal itself to you.

March 14

Your future is waiting for you. Are you
ready to face your fears and meet it?

March 15

If you can love an imperfect person so
perfectly, why can't you love yourself?

March 16

You have to keep visiting the child in you
until you are fully healed and loved.

March 17

Be with those who teach you to live without fear.

March 18

Sometimes you have to be your own inspiration.

March 19

You have to fall so you can learn how to fly.

March 20

What the world needs is more love and compassion.

March 21

All tests in life have an expiry date. Till then,
have hope, keep strong, and be patient.

March 22

Own your insecurities. Then bathe them with
love and light, and watch them disappear.

March 23

Losing someone or something is God's
way of teaching you to let go.

March 24

The person who takes care of everyone is the person who needs to be taken care of the most.

March 25

Love is never lost. It is energy and a force from Allah.

If it comes to you, accept it as a gift, but never
hold on to it. If it goes, know that it was
just temporary and will make its way round
to you again through another person.

Some people are here to love us permanently;
others are only here temporarily.

Very rarely is this in our control.

March 26

Challenge and inspire people to be the best they can be.

March 27

When you are going through your transformation,
like a caterpillar in a cocoon, you will feel a need to
hibernate and close yourself off from the world. Don't
judge yourself or be too hard on yourself. This is your
time. You will need to spend time with yourself whilst
going through this transition. Trust that the people you
love will be there, waiting for you when you emerge.

March 28

When you are feeling down, think of all
the blessings given to you by God the
Most Generous, the Most Kind.

March 29

'And, it was only through art, I discovered who I was.'

March 30

You know when you have found the one
when your heart has found a home.

March 31

Find ease within the hardship and
peace within the struggle.

April

April 1

True love takes time to reveal itself.

April 2

Just live life, and the path will reveal itself.

April 3

Right now, in this moment, I am exactly how God wants me to be, and I am exactly where God wants me to be.

April 4

God would not give you a particular test if he did not think you were capable of passing it.

April 5

Sometimes you have to live the story before you write it.

April 6

Be with a partner you want, not a partner you need. One is love, the other dependency.

April 7

No matter what happens, be patient, and
remember that God loves you.

April 8

Don't wait for all the answers to come to you before you take action. The answers will come to you as you take the next step.

April 9

Some people's hearts never open, and
some people's hearts never close.

April 10

Inspiration doesn't come to you before you take
the path; it comes to you whilst on the path.

April 11

There is nowhere to get to, and nothing to become.
You only need to discover who you already are.

April 12

Sometimes healing comes from sharing your story with one person. Sometimes it comes from sharing your story with the world.

April 13

Life may not always be perfect, but it is always beautiful.

April 14

Find yourself in your words.

April 15

Let life surprise you.

Embrace the unknown.

April 16

Stop trying to fix yourself. You are
perfect the way you are.

April 17

Maybe the best words to hear from a loved one are not 'I love you', but 'I will not give up on you.'

April 18

Be open to the plan of God.

April 19

Sometimes, you inspire people not by
what you do, but by who you are.

April 20

Stop worrying, because God knows what He is doing. It's His plan and you can't control it, but flow with it.

April 21

We pray for success, not realising that success and fame
are also a test. Within every blessing is a test too.

April 22

In dark times, true friends will always be the light.

April 23

It doesn't matter how beautiful the
tree is if the roots are weak.

April 24

Love can heal, because it comes from
God. For those who say it doesn't have
not experienced the true power of it.

April 25

Rejection doesn't mean that your work is not good enough; it means that it is not the right time for your work. Keep going—one day the timing will be right.

April 26

Plant your seeds, then watch your flowers grow.

April 27

It doesn't matter what health condition you
may have, or are currently going through.

Everybody is deserving of love, happiness
and success. Your health condition maybe a
part of you, but it does not define you.

You are so much more than your
condition or your circumstance.

April 28

Float like a leaf. Go where the wind takes you.

April 29

The first step is self-love. The second step is union.

April 30

There is only one way to go: onwards and upwards.

May

May 1

And leave bits of pieces of you wherever you go, because some day, someone will find them and call it treasure.

May 2

'Sometimes my dreams are so big they scare me, but then I think God would not inspire a dream in anyone, if He did not think they were capable of fulfilling it.'

May 3

You only grow old when you stop dreaming.

May 4

Believe in your vision and mission. You are here to do great and extraordinary things.

May 5

You have to start saving yourself
before you start saving others.

May 6

Don't judge your dreams, for they
were inspired by Allah.

May 7

Confidence is like a seed growing a new stalk.
It starts off weak, needing help and support to grow.
Some days you will rise and grow, and
some days you will break and fall.
But, every time you fall, you must plant your
seed again, because every time you fall, the seed
you plant becomes stronger, and one day you
will be strong enough to stand on your own
and the beauty within you will bloom.

May 8

Never let your fear decide your future. Have faith; keep moving. Some dreams are worth chasing for.

May 9

God will give you the answers, when you are ready.

May 10

Sometimes we don't recognise growth
because it looks like struggle.

May 11

When you finally accept all the light and imperfections
in yourself, the path becomes ever clearer.

May 12

You will never know love until you surrender to it.

May 13

'And in stillness, I found my answer.'

May 14

Find comfort in prayer, peace in solitude
and contentment in submission.

May 15

In uncertain times, expect the best.

May 16

Find peace within yourself.

May 17

You can choose to be strong on your own,
or you can be stronger with God.

May 18

'I am not responsible for making other people happy, but for giving other people value.'

May 19

You are already good enough as you are. You are always whole, complete and perfect the way God created you.

May 20

Allah's timing for your success is perfect.

May 21

Focus on intention and leave the outcome to Allah.

May 22

Generosity strengthens your soul.

May 23

Sometimes, God breaks your ego to save your soul.

May 24

Give your heart to the one that
deserves your love the most.

May 25

Don't wait until you are perfect to start making a change in the world. You are already perfect.

May 26

Be the inspiration you seek.

May 27

We can like many people, but we only truly love one.

May 28

Trust your fate. Trust your future.

May 29

'Every situation I am in is always going to be positive, as I can either get through it with patience, or change it through action.'

May 30

Gift people with your presence.

May 31

Breathe. Everything is as it should be.

June

June 1

Inspire people with your inner strength.

June 2

Let your love reach the sky with no boundaries and fear.

June 3

Give life to your soul. Come back to yourself.

June 4

'I am completely and totally lovable.' Repeat.

June 5

Be comfortable with your own truth.

June 6

Where nightmares end, dreams begin.

June 7

Why stand on the shore when you
can dive in the depths?

June 8

Breathe in the sun. Breathe out the sea.

June 9

Loving yourself is an act of gratitude to God.
Every day, strive to love yourself a little more.

June 10

Perfection is an illness where there
is no cure but humbleness.

June 11

The more you love yourself, the
more you can love another.

June 12

'I will shine my light for all to see.'

June 13

With real love, you rise higher than before.

June 14

It's not about showing off your greatness, but sharing it.

June 15

Tell yourself it's okay to feel what you're feeling. Accept your feelings.

June 16

Don't wait until you or the world is ready.
Start chasing your dreams now.

June 17

Love yourself unconditionally, because
that is how God loves you.

June 18

'I am confident and courageous, and I will accomplish all that I set out to do.'

June 19

Shine bright, for God has given you permission to shine His light and show love for His creations.

June 20

What feels like magic to you? Go do that!

June 21

Action leads to clarity.

June 22

Love is the true success.

June 23

'I am grateful for being alive, for being born, for my personality and my character. I am grateful for the inspiration and light that I receive and give to others.'

June 24

'Please be patient.
My wings are being made.'

June 25

Sit in your circle of patience. Let everything you want come to you.

June 26

Moments of happiness come and go. Don't grieve when they go, because they always come back when you don't search for them.

June 27

Share your gifts with the world.

June 28

The light you are searching for has always
been there. It will guide you.

June 29

Sometimes you just have to look fate in the eye, be grateful and accept it.

June 30

'I am here to be the best version of me.'

July

July 1

We all deserve someone who will love us
wholeheartedly and completely.

July 2

Marry someone whose imperfections are perfect for you.

July 3

Learn to distinguish your own thoughts
from the thoughts of others.

July 4

Nature whispers its secrets to those who wish to listen.

July 5

'I have learnt that rarely do people want advice. More often than not they want to be heard and understood.'

July 6

Every moment is purposeful.

July 7

Let go so you can receive.

July 8

When you feel lonely or in darkness, let
your own love shine back to you.

July 9

'I don't know how to be anyone else but me.'

July 10

Learn to be a person of action, not just reflection.

July 11

Remember, God rewards your intentions.

July 12

Just because you failed once doesn't mean
you will fail again. Maybe it wasn't your
time then, but it's your time now.

July 13

There is a difference between saying thank you with your heart and saying thank you with your words.

July 14

You are where you are in life because
of someone or another.

Don't forget to thank God for all the people
in your life who truly are a blessing.

July 15

Sometimes you need to think simple, because the answer, more often than not, is simple.

July 16

Wisdom comes with age. Wisdom comes from experience, but the best wisdom comes from mistakes.

July 17

Some people never give up on love,
and those are the brave ones.

July 18

So when the time comes, be patient
and let your heart lead the way.

July 19

Sometimes, it's more important to know how you feel than what you think.

July 20

Do not look for a partner to complete you, because no human can complete another. Look for a partner who complements you, who can add value to what you have already got.

July 21

Wait for the one who loves like you do. Life's too short to settle for anything else.

July 22

Some people wait for a miracle. Others create them.

July 23

Let your heart beat to the drum of its own soul.

July 24

You search for beauty around you, yet the
source of all beauty lies within you.

July 25

Embrace all that you are, and fall in love with it.

July 26

When you're struggling, don't demand more of yourself. Be gentle on yourself and pray more. God will surely help you through.

July 27

There is an art in falling, and there
is an art in getting back up.

July 28

They say love can move mountains, and the first mountain you have to move is yourself.

July 29

Those who rush to success fail to stop and see
the real beauty of success—the journey.

July 30

Learn the importance of accepting compliments
as easily as you have learnt to give them.

July 31

Never compare where you are in life with someone else. Your journey is not the same as theirs, and neither is your destination.

August

August 1

Intelligence isn't intelligence without compassion.

August 2

Every day, you are getting one step closer
to your path and your purpose.

August 3

Remember, the past does not exist, so stop living in it.

August 4

Believe that there is a God that is taking care of you.

August 5

Self-growth comes from a place of self-acceptance.

August 6

You don't search for happiness. Happiness is always around you. You open yourself to it, and let it come find you.

August 7

If in doubt, remember God knows what He is doing.

August 8

Do not be afraid of people's judgement of yourself.

Remember, God is the higher judge.

August 9

Start small, think big—but start.

August 10

Get comfortable with being a human, having
weaknesses and making mistakes, but knowing
you're always learning and growing.

August 11

Remember: if it's easy, you flow.
If it's difficult, you grow.

August 12

You can never lose something that was
never destined to be yours.

August 13

There isn't anybody on earth who can wear your shoes and walk your path.

August 14

Let go of your need to fix others, and work on
improving yourself. Let God deal with the rest.

August 15

Sometimes it's the smallest acts done on a
consistent basis that change the world.

August 16

'It might not make much sense now, but
everything will make sense one day, I promise.'

August 17

Don't look for heaven on earth.
Work for heaven on earth.

August 18

Yes, you DO matter. The work you do matters.
The words you express matter. Your silence
matters. Your presence matters. Your absence
matters. Your thoughts matter. Your love
matters. Everything about you matters.

August 19

Just because you are a sensitive soul does not make you a weak soul. It takes strength to feel things so very deeply.

August 20

When the world gets tough, drive through
the storm. Trust that you will find your
way to brighter and clearer days.

August 21

If you write just one truth about
yourself, you set yourself free.

August 22

'And it's amazing what the right intentions
and hard work can achieve.'

August 23

Life will keep on bringing you to the same place.
Deep down, you know the reason why.

August 24

'And I finally realised that being hard on myself
never got me very far, so I became gentle instead.'

August 25

God will surely help you along the way, no
matter what obstacles come along.

August 26

If you ever feel like giving up, find a
greater purpose than yourself.

August 27

'So I learnt the hard way that it is much better to fulfil silent promises than to break loud, open promises.'

August 28

Don't strive to please others first, strive to please God.
You are here to please God, and not people.

August 29

If you had a dark past, then know that it's because
God wishes for you a brighter and bigger future.

August 30

If you believe in it, you will do it.

August 31

You may have suffered, but you have survived. That is why you are your own greatest hero alive.

September

September 1

Failure comes from giving up too soon.

September 2

Go climb that mountain and shout to the world
who you are and what you're made of.

September 3

The best way to see the world is through your
own eyes, and not through someone else's.

September 4

Ask yourself: do you want to change something that you want to be part of, or do want to create something that you want to be a part of?

September 5

Just as a good word is an act of kindness,
so is refraining from a bad word.

September 6

There is no such thing as failure, just God
pointing you to another direction.

September 7

Be kind to your heart and stop worrying about
the things that are out of your control.

September 8

The greatest obstacles are not the ones
you face, but the ones you create.

September 9

Remember, feelings don't need to be fixed
or understood, just acknowledged.

September 10

Be kind to yourself. Sometimes the person that most deserves your kindness is yourself.

September 11

Living a life with kindness, love and purpose is
the best legacy that one can leave behind.

September 12

It's not about winning or losing. It's about developing and growing.

September 13

Do not wait until your life is perfect to be happy.

September 14

Maybe we don't need to fight for our dreams,
but allow them to gently appear.

September 15

You can still be happy despite facing
challenges and hardships. Happiness does
not lie in perfection, it lies in peace.

September 16

Maybe we are so focused on our own worries
that we fail to notice other people's pain.

September 17

To seek perfection is a natural desire. But to seek it in this imperfect world is foolish.

September 18

'I am still waiting for that day, when I do
more than think and talk, for it is thought
followed by action that leads to change.'

September 19

What you desire has already been created.

September 20

Don't be too hard on yourself. Be your own best friend, and not your own worst enemy.

September 21

Let your wounded soul heal in its own time. Do not set it a time limit. This stops the soul from healing.

September 22

Don't hide your darkness, because only when you bring it to the light can it be removed.

September 23

'And just when you are about to give up on life, you will meet that person who will be your every reason not to.'

September 24

Success doesn't always come from having the greatest childhood. So, don't let the past deceive you.

September 25

It takes great strength to believe in what you can't see or feel in the present moment. Have fearless faith in your dreams.

September 26

Sometimes the greatest work being done
is the work you never hear about.

September 27

Life can make us cynics. Because of this, we miss many opportunities that could have turned our cynicism upside down.

If we did not have the option to work for someone else's dream, we would have no choice but to work for our own.

September 29

'And it's sad when you can see the light in someone, but they can't see it in themselves. The only thing you can do is keep shining until they realise the light they see in you is a reflection of them.'

September 30

Sometimes we have to travel the wrong
path to appreciate the right path.

October

October 1

You can inspire someone and support someone, but you can't change anyone. The desire to change can only from within.

October 2

It takes great strength to admit that life is better when you have someone to share life's storms together.

October 3

Why live in the past, when the future is waiting for you?

October 4

You were born too extra-ordinary
to live an ordinary life.

October 5

Nobody can bring out something in you which you didn't have all along. The truth is you had it in you all along, but you couldn't see it until someone saw it in you.

October 6

Every time you write, you are planting a seed, so continue to write and one day your writing will bloom.

October 7

You can choose to live your heart like a rose or a thorn. You can choose to expose its beauty, or be the thorn that protects it. But whether you expose the heart or not, one day it will wither, so you might as well take the risk and expose it.

October 8

Nothing is ever truly lost if it yours by destiny.

October 9

Kindness is not weakness. It is the most beautiful kind of courage there is.

October 10

Time spent finding out who you really are
and your purpose is never wasted.

October 11

Passionate people are simply people who
feel too much about everything.

October 12

Think of everything you have and
not of what you don't have.

October 13

Be the best imperfect person you can be.

October 14

Marry someone you respect.

October 15

The right person cannot complete you, but they
can guide you to the source which can: God.

October 16

Sometimes, we really need to humble ourselves and accept that God's plans are better than our own plans.

October 17

Have hope in God. He wants the best for you always.

October 18

It's not what comes to you that gives you true
fulfilment, but what comes from you.

October 19

Wake up and praise God. You are blessed,
you are alive. You are loved, and you will
have a great day, God willing.

October 20

Take care of your present, and God
will take care of your future.

October 21

Let your heart be the muscle that you use the most.

October 22

If you stop trying to be like others, you
will find the beauty of being yourself.

October 23

There are gems at the bottom of the ocean waiting
for you. If only you are brave enough to dive!

October 24

Every day, try and find something new about yourself.

October 25

It's okay to take time to grow your wings.
The longer you take, the stronger your
wings and the further you will fly.

October 26

In the end, it is not about how much love you
received, but how much love you gave.

October 27

Let go of the labels you incorrectly give yourself.

October 28

'How long did I work for my dream, and how long did I work for someone else's dream?'

October 29

Focus on who you are, not on what you are not.
Focus on all you have, not on what you don't have.
Focus on your blessings, not on your pain.
Focus on your successes, not on your failures.

Focus on the direction in which you wish to
go, not on the place where you are now.
Focus on what is going right in your
life, not on what is going wrong.

October 30

Forgiveness sets you free. Acceptance helps you grow.

October 31

Step up, one step at a time.

November

November 1

Blessings can be found in pain. Success within failure. Healing within patience. Contentment within chaos. Wholeness within emptiness.

November 2

Life is a journey. You just have to travel
it and trust it as best as you can.

November 3

You will find what you are looking for,
because it has always been within you.

November 4

It takes great strength to travel your
own path and not someone else's.

November 5

True love doesn't hurt; unrequited love hurts.

November 6

Think of the best-case scenario, not
the worst-case scenario.

November 7

We succeed, we fail. We make mistakes, we learn and we grow. It's all part of the journey.

November 8

Prayer is God's gift to you. A taste of
sweetness, faith and submission.

November 9

Don't try to be anything but yourself.

November 10

You don't need to be rich and successful in this world to please God. You just need good intentions, good actions and good deeds.

November 11

What you give always comes back,
sometimes sooner rather than later.

November 12

Becoming an adult is like crossing a bridge, split
halfway. To get to the other side you have to jump.
This jump takes faith, patience, self-love and self-belief.
Some people will move faster than others, but the
important thing is not to rush, but not to avoid it either.

It will always be ready for you when you are.
Take the time to grow your wings, your
inner strength and courage.
Find yourself, find God, and when you
are ready, take that jump and fly.

November 13

Stop, relax, and stop chasing the future.

Where you are is where you are supposed to be.

Enjoy the present moment. The
future will come on its own.

Prepare for it; don't chase it.

November 14

If you want help, help others.

November 15

Appreciate the blessings you have whilst you
have them, and not when they're gone.

November 16

Sometimes we focus so much on what we don't have, we lose focus on what we do have.

November 17

'And it's true that if we search deep within
ourselves, we find out who we are.'

November 18

Be thankful for your weaknesses, for your own weaknesses teach you humbleness.

November 19

By being kind to yourself, you give
yourself the space you need to grow.

November 20

Focus on your own faults, so you don't
have time to seek faults of others.

November 21

Think of all the things that have gone right in your
life and where God has helped you through.

November 22

Stop trying to be something, and start creating
and doing something meaningful instead.

November 23

Accomplish things not because you
have to, but because you want to.

November 24

Your worth comes from God, not from people.
To God, you are worth more than you think.

November 25

Where do your dreams come from? Do
they come from fear or out of love?
The ones that come from love are the
real dreams worth fighting for.

November 26

The ego is always hungry, whereas the soul is always full.

November 27

Let go of who you think you need to be, and let God show you the path that leads to who you are meant to be.

November 28

'I am not afraid of being alone, because
I am never alone. I have God.'

November 29

You have to accept yourself, because
your acceptance matters the most.

November 30

You can think as much as you like, but thinking alone does not lead to change, action or success. It's thought followed by action that creates change.

December

December 1

Don't strive to become—just be.

December 2

When you feel like you need to heal and make a move, that's a sign your wings have grown bigger than the place you are in, and you need to move to a place big enough for you to spread your wings and grow.

December 3

When you try too hard to create with
your mind, you fail. When you try to
create from your soul, you succeed.

December 4

The bravest person is the person who is not afraid
to ask for help when needed, and show that
they are not 'Superwoman' or 'Superman'.

December 5

Where you are now is not where you will always be.
Change is constant, and moments are temporary.

December 6

If you don't love yourself, how can you love
the one that created you? Love yourself, so
you can love the One that created you.

December 7

Give your heart to God, and He will
protect it for the right person.

December 8

Don't be sad when things come to an end,
because a new chapter is about to begin.

December 9

You can't hate yourself into a better person.

December 10

There is nothing you can't do with God's help.

December 11

Your dreams have always been waiting for you.
Will you be bold and take a step towards them?

December 12

It always works out the way it was intended to.

December 13

To be vulnerable is to be human. Take risks. Be
brave. Show the world who you really are.

December 14

In the end, we fall in love with a person's heart and soul.

December 15

It is better to make a wrong decision and learn something from it, than never make a decision and learn nothing at all.

December 16

God speaks to you through His signs.

December 17

If Allah wants great from you, He will test you.
Every test serves a purpose till its appointed time.

December 18

You can be as happy as you dream to be.

December 19

Don't love the gift more than the giver.

December 20

'I think we are all looking for someone who
makes us feel our most authentic selves.'

December 21

Leave your mark; leave your legacy.

December 22

I accept, embrace and celebrate my destiny
and God's plan, which is perfect for me.

December 23

With faith and patience, anything is possible.

December 24

Whenever you feel afraid, just remember
your dream, and that God is taking care of
you and wishes the best for you always.

December 25

There is no darkness that light cannot overpower.
Rise like the sun. The light will always shine brighter.

December 26

You are what the world is waiting for.
Keep going, for your next step
could be your masterpiece.

December 27

Your soul becomes weak by taking,
and strong by giving.

Give to yourself first, so you can give to another.

December 28

Knowledge is given to you to inspire, and then to share.

December 29

Any opportunity to help is a gift from God.

December 30

You do not look for love. It is within you. You
awaken yourself to love, and let it find you.

December 31

Serving others brings life to your soul,
and in it lies your unique purpose.

Acknowledgements

First and foremost all praise belongs to Allah.

Secondly, I am grateful and thankful to my family, friends, coaches and mentors who have supported me and guided me throughout this writing journey. This book would not have been possible without the loving help and support that I received.

To my mother and grandad who made this dream possible.

To my beautiful sister for her editing, advice and guidance. (Thank you for your patience!)

To my best friends, cousins, and family members who encouraged me with my dreams. (you know who you all are!)

Finally, to all my readers and supporters. Thank you for your support, love and presence.

May God bless you all!

xx

Further Information

Connect

www.facebook.com/aneshareflects
www.aneshareflects.wordpress.com
www.instagram.com/aneshareflects

Author Biography

Anesha Pandor is an inspirational writer, poet and life coach. She writes to inspire others to follow and fulfil their dreams, and to help others discover the beauty and miracle of themselves. She also enjoys travelling and is passionate about the arts and creative expression.

Lightning Source UK Ltd.
Milton Keynes UK
UKOW04f1410160118
316245UK00001B/7/P